ANIMAL FAMILIES

GORILLAS
LIFE IN THE TROOP

Willow Clark

PowerKiDS
press™

New York

Published in 2011 by The Rosen Publishing Group, Inc.
29 East 21st Street, New York, NY 10010

First Edition

Editor: Jennifer Way
Book Design: Julio Gil

Photo Credits: Cover, pp. 10–11, 17, 19, 21, 24 (top right) Shutterstock.com; back cover © www. iStockphoto.com/Kristijan Hranisavljevic; pp. 5, 24 (bottom right) Hemera/Thinkstock; p. 7 Photos.com/ Thinkstock; pp. 9, 12–13, 24 (bottom left) iStockphoto/Thinkstock; pp. 15, 24 (top left) Andy Rouse/Getty Images; p. 23 Andrew Plumptre/Getty Images.

Library of Congress Cataloging-in-Publication Data

Clark, Willow.
  Gorillas : life in the troop / by Willow Clark. — 1st ed.
    p. cm. — (Animal families)
  Includes bibliographical references and index.
  ISBN 978-1-4488-2514-1 (library binding) — ISBN 978-1-4488-2614-8 (pbk.) —
ISBN 978-1-4488-2615-5 (6-pack)
  1. Gorilla—Juvenile literature. 2. Familial behavior in animals—Juvenile literature. I. Title.
  QL737.P96C58 2011
  599.884—dc22
                                        2010019393

Manufactured in the United States of America

CPSIA Compliance Information: Batch #WW11PK: For Further Information contact Rosen Publishing, New York, New York at 1-800-237-9932

CONTENTS

Gorillas live in Africa. A family of gorillas is called a **troop**.

Troops have one or two young males. Troops also have females and their young.

An older male gorilla is the troop leader. He is called the **silverback**.

9

The silverback is the biggest and strongest of all the gorillas in the troop.

Gorillas spend most of their day looking for food. They eat plants, bugs, and worms.

When the troop is resting, the members **groom** each other.

Each member of the troop makes a sleeping **nest**. Mother gorillas hold their babies.

Baby gorillas ride on their mothers' backs for the first two or three years of their lives.

Young gorillas play while their mothers watch them.

Gorillas leave the troop when they are 8 to 11 years old. They join a new troop.

Words to Know

groom

nest

silverback

troop

Index

Web Sites

Due to the changing nature of Internet links, PowerKids Press has developed an online list of Web sites related to the subject of this book. This site is updated regularly. Please use this link to access the list:

www.powerkidslinks.com/afam/gorilla/

24